To the farmers of America —T.B.

Dedicated to the memory of my hardworking
grandpa William H. Thomas —D.T.

THIS IS A BORZOI BOOK PUBLISHED BY ALFRED A. KNOPF

Text copyright © 2018 by Tonya Bolden
Jacket art and interior illustrations copyright © 2018 by Don Tate

All rights reserved. Published in the United States by Alfred A. Knopf, an imprint of
Random House Children's Books, a division of Penguin Random House LLC, New York.

Knopf, Borzoi Books, and the colophon are registered trademarks of Penguin Random House LLC.

Visit us on the Web! rhcbooks.com

Educators and librarians, for a variety of teaching tools, visit us at RHTeachersLibrarians.com

Library of Congress Cataloging-in-Publication Data is available upon request.

ISBN 978-0-385-75276-3 (trade) — ISBN 978-0-385-75277-0 (lib. bdg.) — ISBN 978-0-385-75278-7 (ebook)

The text of this book is set in 15-point Latienne.
The illustrations were created using mixed media.

MANUFACTURED IN CHINA
October 2018
10 9 8 7 6

First Edition

Random House Children's Books supports the First Amendment and celebrates the right to read.

NO SMALL POTATOES

Junius G. Groves and His
Kingdom in Kansas

by **Tonya Bolden**
illustrated by **Don Tate**

ALFRED A. KNOPF

New York

ONE POTATO.
TWO POTATO.
THIRTY-ELEVEN MILLION POTATOES?

Is that how many potatoes
Junius George Groves grew?

No, not thirty-eleven million, not exactly.
But he—"Junius G.," for short—he sure
grew piles and piles of spuds. So many
that he was crowned the Potato King—
a legend known far and wide.

Folks were doubly amazed when they heard about Junius G.'s bleak beginnings in the Bluegrass State.

No crown. No kingdom. Not an inch of ground. When baby Junius G. first laid eyes on the world, he had nothing to call his own. Legally, not even himself. He was born into slavery, on a plantation near Greensburg, Kentucky.

Thank goodness, Junius G. didn't stay in slavery for a long, long time. He was yet young when freedom came. That happened when America abolished slavery, in late 1865.

Junius G. didn't stay in the Bluegrass State for a long, long time, either. In 1879, when he was about twenty, he left, taking part in an ever-growing exodus: a great going-out, a great going-away.

I worked around for planters here and there and managed to pick up a little reading and figuring in a log schoolhouse at Columbia, Kentucky.

—Junius G., in 1905

From Kentucky, Tennessee, and other Southern states, tens of thousands of people, most country folk and a host with youngsters in tow, shook the dust from their feet.

"Exodusters," they were called.

With hearts hugging hope, clutching dreams of bountiful lives, Exodusters went west, to the Plains. Land was plentiful there, they heard. For many, that place of promise was Kansas, the Sunflower State.

Exodusters journeyed by steamboat, by train, in bumpety-bump oxcarts, in wide-wheeled wagons. Some of those keen on Kansas put down roots in new towns like Nicodemus. Others settled in or near Topeka and Kansas City. Both these burgs were along the Kansas River, also known as the Kaw.

As for Exoduster Junius G., they say that he walked to Kansas, more than five hundred miles. Along the way, he worked odd jobs.

Junius G. ended his journey in the Great Kaw Valley: in a part of Kansas City, Kansas, bound by an oxbow bend in the Kaw. This place was soon called Armourdale. There, Junius G. landed a job on a potato farm.

For a lowly forty cents a day.

Junius G. could so easily have pitied himself over his piddling pay, but he didn't. Instead, he made up his mind to just work hard.

A few moons later, Junius G. got a raise in pay—to seventy-five cents a day! And he kept working hard—so hard that the man for whom he worked, J. T. Williamson, made him foreman of his farm. With that came another raise: fifty more cents a day.

It was several weeks before I could get work on a farm, and when I finally did secure a place, it was at almost starvation wages, 40 cents per day. . . . This was better than being forced to roam the streets and beg, so I gladly accepted the offer, determined to work my way up to better things. By keeping my eyes open, always attending to duty and doing more, rather than less, than was required of me, I soon succeeded in having my wages raised.

—Junius G., in 1900

Still, Junius G. wanted more—and not just more money. He dreamed of farming for himself. Lacking the bucks to buy some land, he did the next best thing: he rented land from J. T. Williamson. Nine acres. For use of his land, his tools, and his team, Junius G. agreed to pay J.T. with a share of the crops.

Junius G. planted white potatoes on one-third of those nine acres.

In time, Junius G. was renting twenty acres, then sixty-six acres, growing more and more spuds. And he kept hoping for a farm of his own.

Hoping alongside him was Matilda E. Stewart, the woman he married about a year after he reached Kansas. Just like Junius G., Matilda E. was no lazybones. She didn't hiccup and holler at the hint of hard work.

With Matilda E. his steady, sturdy helpmate, Junius G. kept working hard, day after day, dawn to dusk. Come true-dark, the couple slept away a day's weary in a one-room shack.

Week after week, Junius G. and Matilda E. put off purchasing trifles and trinkets. They only bought needful things. That way they could save up every spare dollar, dime, nickel. Every spare penny, too! This money came from the crops they sold and from other work they did on the side, such as chopping firewood in winter to sell to townsfolk.

All that working and saving up paid off! In late 1884, Junius G. had his eye on eighty acres. This land was east of Edwardsville, near the mouth of the Kaw, its banks lined with cottonwood trees.

Junius G. and Matilda E. had saved up twenty-two hundred dollars, but those eighty acres near Edwardsville cost *thirty-six hundred dollars*. Where would the fourteen-hundred-dollar difference come from? The wind? A cloud? Some magic tree?

No siree! It would come from hard work—that's what Junius G. believed when he handed over those twenty-two hundred bucks.

With it was the promise to pay off the balance in a year.

Right quick, Junius G. went to work turning those eighty acres into a real farm. There was a small house to build. More daunting than that was the back-straining, muscle-taxing task of clearing the land. For starters, digging up umpteen tree stumps—so many as to make for stepping-stones up and down a field.

And while Junius G. was doing all that, the top crop on his mind?

POTATOES!

But could he do it? Could he farm hard
enough to pay off the money he still
owed on those eighty acres? In a year?
If he didn't, he was liable to lose the land
and those twenty-two hundred bucks.

Negative natterings of naysaying neighbors snaked their way to Junius G.'s ears. He did a dumb deal, these people humphed. He would never pay off that debt in a year, they tut-tutted. When they looked into Junius G.'s future, those naysaying neighbors saw nothing but failure.

PRODUCE

The negative natterings kicked up a ruckus in Junius G.'s head, made him sad, scared, down, discouraged. It wasn't like he had only *himself* to worry about. There was Matilda E. What's more, the couple had three young sons by then: Charles, Walter, and Fred, stair-step kids.

Maybe those neighbors were right, feared
Junius G. Maybe he had dreamed too big—
bitten off more than he could chew.

What to do?

KEEP WORKING HARD!

Planting.
Plowing.
Tilling.
Hilling.
Hoping for right rain.

Watching potato vines grow,
then waiting for their blooms.

Keeping his courage up under
searing sun, in the face of hot,
heavy winds.

Plus, Junius G. had to be ever ready to battle blister beetles, roly-polies, and other potato pests.

Come harvest time—more hard work!

Working hard worked! True to his word, Junius G. paid off the money he owed in a year.

It was pretty risky business paying out every dollar we had saved by five years' hard work and close living and running ourselves $1,400 in debt, but we wanted a home of our own . . . and I knew that I should succeed much better when I was tilling soil that I could call my own.
—Junius G., in 1900

Once those eighty acres were really his, can you guess what Junius G. decided to do?

KEEP WORKING HARD!

In time, Junius G. bought more land in the Great Kaw Valley. All told, more than five hundred acres. And year after year, he kept working hard.

So hard that in 1894, the *Kansas Blackman* called him the "Potato King" of his county, which was Wyandotte.

So hard that in 1900, the *Indianapolis Recorder* hailed him the "Potato King" of the whole Sunflower State.

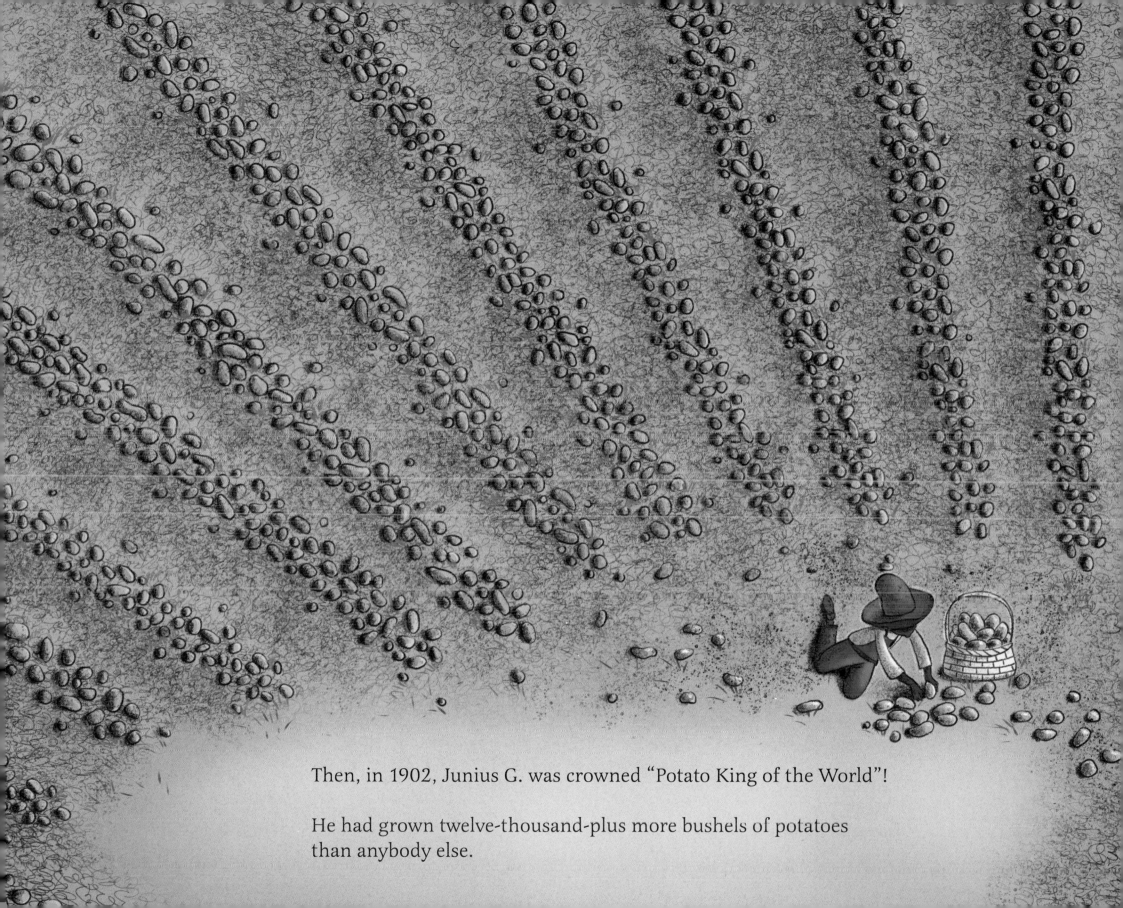

Then, in 1902, Junius G. was crowned "Potato King of the World"!

He had grown twelve-thousand-plus more bushels of potatoes than anybody else.

How many potatoes had Junius George Groves grown that year?

Seventy-two thousand one hundred and fifty bushels—or about four million pounds of spuds. Put another way: roughly twelve million potatoes!

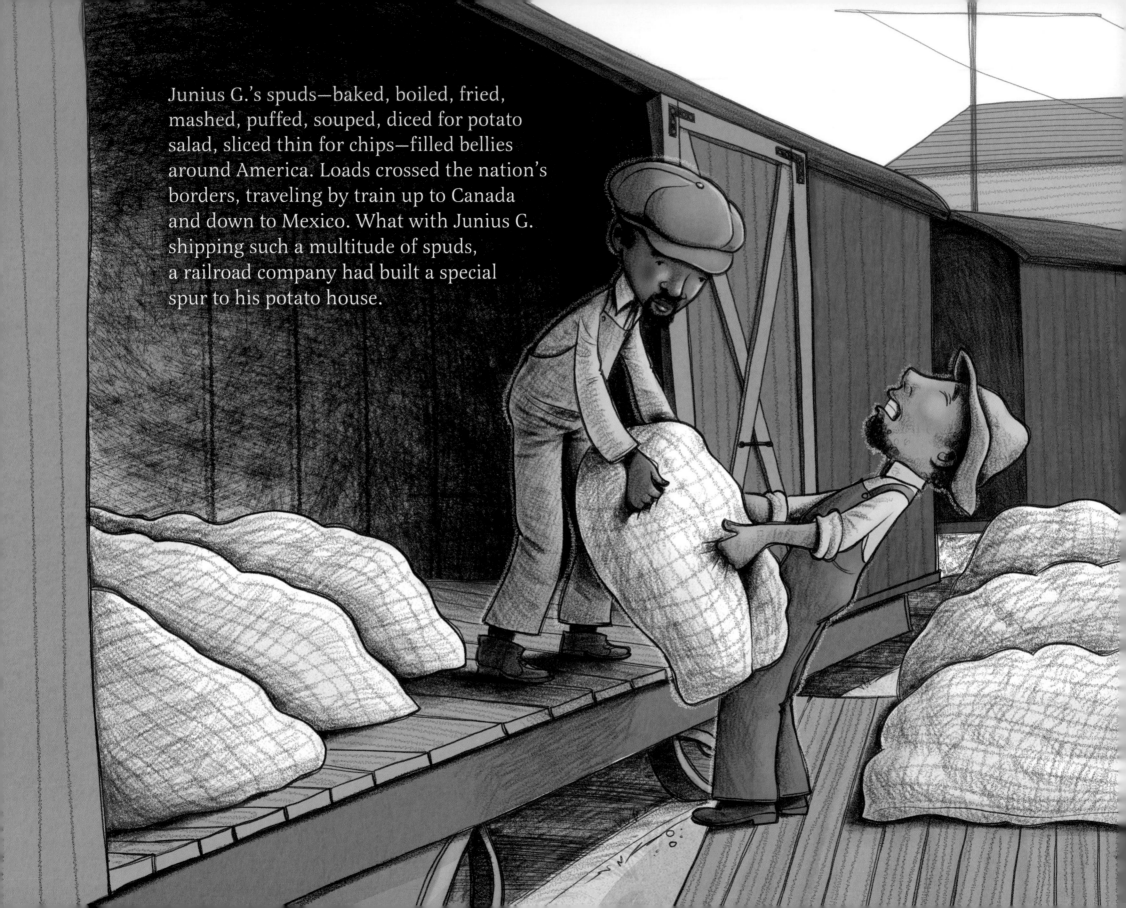

Junius G.'s spuds—baked, boiled, fried, mashed, puffed, souped, diced for potato salad, sliced thin for chips—filled bellies around America. Loads crossed the nation's borders, traveling by train up to Canada and down to Mexico. What with Junius G. shipping such a multitude of spuds, a railroad company had built a special spur to his potato house.

Even after all the fame, farmer Junius G. kept working hard, kept loving his rich dark earth—likening the furrows his plows churned up to "chocolate waves."

While all those spuds grew year after year, so, too, did Junius G.'s family. A dozen little Groveses were born and raised to full-grown on their parents' farm.

As Charles, Walter, Fred, Ora, Ida Mae, Lillian, Junius G. Jr., Sylvester, Etna, John, Cornelius, and Theodore grew, they, too, learned the land: the hundreds of acres planted in potatoes; the parcels sown with other crops, like cabbage and carrots and corn. There were fruit trees, too.

So here we are: every one of my boys a farmer; every one of my girls married to a farmer; every man and boy of them in overalls and working hard. . . . I want these boys and girls of mine to stay on the land. . . . I want my children and grandchildren always to be able to stand up and say: "We are a part and parcel of that army of farmers which feeds America!"

—Junius G., in 1919

Over the years, the Potato King grew more than a big family, more than cabbage and carrots and corn, more than fruit trees. More than potatoes.

Junius G. grew jobs—hiring farmhands. Junius G. grew a park—Groves Park. And a cozy community—Groves Center. And a church—Pleasant Hill Baptist. A store that sold groceries and other goods. A golf course, too.

Junius G. also built bigger and bigger homes for his family. The last one was a twenty-two-room red-brick mansion. It had white-stone trim, a red-tile roof, and strong oak doors.

A most marvelous room behind those doors was a ballroom, which doubled as a play palace when Junius G.'s children were young.

The library was perhaps Junius G.'s favorite room, so full of books and booklets on every facet of farming—books and booklets he called his "college." Along with all the acres he tilled. Along with all the food he grew.

And dawn to dusk, on any given day—winter, spring, summer, fall—Junius G., the Potato King, could behold his Kaw Valley kingdom from the veranda of that red-brick mansion, with its white-stone trim, red-tile roof, and strong oak doors—his castle!

FROM THE LIFE AND TIMES OF JUNIUS G.

October 1843 Junius G.'s parents, Mary and Martin, marry on a plantation on the Green River's Caney Fork, near Greensburg, Kentucky. The plantation belongs to Alfred Anderson, a former member of the U.S. Congress and one of the largest slaveholders in the area. Junius G.'s father is held in slavery by William Grove, whose plantation is near Anderson's.

May 13, 1858 In a late-1860s affidavit, Alfred Anderson stated that Junius G. was born on this day. He is the seventh of the nine children his parents will have. Several twentieth-century sources give Junius G.'s birthday as April 12, 1859, and at least one article quotes him as saying that he was born in 1861.

April 9, 1865 The Civil War, which began in April 1861, is essentially over when, in Appomattox, Virginia, the Confederacy's leading general, Robert E. Lee, surrenders to the Union's leading general, Ulysses S. Grant.

April 22, 1865 Junius G.'s father, age forty-four, joins the U.S. Army at Lebanon, Kentucky. He is in Company G of the 125th Regiment Infantry U.S. Colored Troops.

On or about May 6, 1865 Junius G.'s father dies near Louisville, Kentucky, aboard a hospital ship on the Ohio River. Two comrades later state that it was generally believed that Martin Grove and several other soldiers died as a result of eating poisoned pies purchased from a vendor. They also said that Martin Grove had been "a stout, hearty man possessed of strong and vigorous physical powers."

December 6, 1865 The Thirteenth Amendment to the Constitution, abolishing slavery in America, is ratified.

November 28, 1868 As Martin Grove's widow, Junius G.'s mother begins receiving a pension of $8 a month from the U.S. government (payments to end in March 1879). Junius G. and four siblings are to receive $2 a month until they turn sixteen. In pension-related documents, the family's last name is given as "Grove" and as "Groves." Clearly at some point Junius G. settled on "Groves."

June 7, 1870 According to the federal census, Junius G., several siblings, their mother, and their stepfather, farmer Henry Cox, live in Haskinsville, in Green County, Kentucky. Also in the household, a baby boy named Walker and a seventeen-year-old named William.

March 29, 1879 Junius G. leaves Kentucky with $1.25.

May 9, 1880 Junius G. marries Matilda E., who was born in Wellington, Missouri, in February 1863.

April 14, 1881 The Groveses' son Charles is born in Armourdale, Kansas. The couple will have many more children (the last one born in 1903), but not all will live into adulthood.

September 19, 1891 An item on page 2 of the *Historic Times* (Lawrence, Kansas) reports that Junius G. and H. P. Ewing (of Loring, Kansas) are two of the richest black men in Kansas.

March 1, 1895 Junius G. has 400 acres in potatoes, according to the Kansas State Agricultural Census. Other crops include corn (160 acres), apple trees (170), and cherry trees (50). Livestock includes nine horses, two cows, and twenty-four pigs.

September 1899 Oldest son Charles enters Kansas State Agricultural College in Manhattan, Kansas, at a time when less than 15 percent of Americans have a high school diploma.

March 29, 1900 An item on page 4 of the Oshkosh *Daily Northwestern* calls Groves Park "one of the most picturesque spots in Wyandotte County." At the time, the Groves family lives in a fourteen-room house.

April 21, 1900 An item on page 4 of the *Indianapolis Recorder* reports that Junius G. is believed to be the richest black man "living between the Missouri River and the Rockies."

June 7, 1901 An item on page 1 of the *Topeka Plaindealer* urges, "Don't forget the 'Cross Road Grocery Store,' owned and controlled by J.G. Groves. Mr. Groves is doing a business worthy of anybody's attention."

1902 Junius G. is crowned "Potato King of the World" in Helsinki, Finland. The honor is bestowed upon him by the United States Department of Agriculture and presented by the Carnegie Steel Company.

June 1904 Son Charles graduates from Kansas State Agricultural College. Several siblings also attend the college or its preparatory school, but Charles is the only one to graduate.

June 29, 1906 An item on page 1 in the *Topeka Plaindealer* reports on the first-annual meeting of the Sunflower State Agricultural Society at Groves Center. Junius G. co-founded this organization. Son Charles is president; daughter Ida Mae is secretary. (Groves Center was the community Junius G. founded.)

May 26, 1909 An item on page 4 of the *Kansas City* (Missouri) *Star* reports on the construction of Junius G.'s twenty-two-room mansion.

May 15, 1910 An item on page 12A of the *Kansas City* (Missouri) *Star* reports that Junius G. recently sold eighty acres of his Kaw Valley land, leaving him with 523 acres. On these acres are seven "large and comfortable" farmhouses for hired hands.

December 13, 1919 An item that begins on page 8 of the *Country Gentleman* magazine reports that Junius G. and Matilda E.'s remaining eleven sons and daughters live on the farm, along with nine sons- and daughters-in-law and eight grandchildren. Junius G. still has roughly 500 acres of land in the Kaw Valley. Other real-estate holdings include 1,600 acres of "fine wheat land" in Gove County (in northwest Kansas). Junius G. told the magazine that his Gove County land was purchased for the "overflow of Groveses."

August 17, 1925 Junius George Groves dies in his mid-sixties (whether he was born in 1858, 1859, or 1861).

August 21, 1930 Matilda E. Groves dies at the age of sixty-six.

August 8–9, 2007 Junius Groves Days is established by proclamation of the city of Edwardsville, Kansas. The celebration includes a reenactment of the agreement between Junius G. and Union Pacific Railroad to construct a spur to his farm.

GLOSSARY

acre a measurement of land equal to 43,560 square feet.

blister beetle an insect that can devour potato leaves and produces a substance that causes blisters on a person's skin.

bushel a unit of volume for dry measure equal to 2,150 cubic inches. Also, a vessel with that capacity, as in a bushel basket.

Exodusters the name given to black people who left the South for the Plains in the 1870s and 1880s in search of a better life.

foreman a person in charge of a crew of workers.

furrow a long, narrow trench, or rut, usually made with a plow.

helpmate a good buddy and helper. Also, a spouse.

hill to draw soil around the roots or base.

oxbow bend a U-shaped bend or curve in a body of water.

piddling small.

spud a nickname for the potato. "Tater" and "earth apple" are two others.

spur a short stretch of train track that branches off the main line.

till to prepare land for growing crops, as by plowing. Also, to weed.

NOTES

"I worked around . . .": "Negro Business Men in Convention," *St. Louis Republic*, August 17, 1905, 3.

"It was several . . .": "A Potato King," *Topeka Plaindealer*, May 4, 1900, 1.

"It was pretty risky . . .": "A Potato King," *Topeka Plaindealer*, May 4, 1900, 1.

Junius G. named Potato King of the World: Correspondence from Angela Doyle Radicia.

"chocolate waves": "By the Sweat of His Face," *The Country Gentleman*, December 13, 1919, 8.

"So here we are . . .": "By the Sweat of His Face," *The Country Gentleman*, December 13, 1919, 8.

"college": "By the Sweat of His Face," *The Country Gentleman*, December 13, 1919, 56.

"a stout, hearty man . . .": Pension File.

SELECTED SOURCES

Anders, Tisa M. "Groves, Junius George (1859–1925)." www.blackpast.org/aaw/groves-junius-george-1859-1925.

Angus, Donald. "By the Sweat of His Face," *The Country Gentleman*, December 13, 1919, 8, 56, 58.

Babyak, Jolene, and Kathy Hoggard. "A Black Man's Kingdom in Kansas," *Kansas City Times*, November 22, 1972, 26.

Daily Northwestern. "The Potato Trust," March 29, 1900, 4 (picked up from the *Kansas City Journal*).

Dunbar, Paul Laurence. "Representative American Negroes," *The Negro Problem*, New York: James Pott & Co., 1903, 187–209.

Groves, Junius George. Will and related documents in Probate File #13474.

Hawkins, Anne P. W. "Hoeing Their Own Row: Black Agriculture and the Agrarian Ideal in Kansas, 1880–1920," *Kansas History*, Autumn 1999, 200–13.

Indianapolis Freeman. "City and Society," December 19, 1908, 8.

Indianapolis Recorder. "General Race News," April 21, 1900, 4.

Kansas Blackman. "Locals," June 8, 1894, 7.

Kansas City (Missouri) *Star*. "How This Negro Farmer Rose from Slavery to Wealth," May 15, 1910, 12A.

Kansas State Agricultural College Yearbook, Sunrise, 1904.

Mather, Frank Lincoln, ed. *Who's Who of the Colored Race: A General Biographical Dictionary of Men and Women of African Descent*, vol. 1. n.p.: Chicago, IL, 1915.

National Archives and Records Administration. Compiled Military Service File for Martin Grove and Federal Military Pension Application File for Martin Grove (application #125246) Federal Military Pension.

Painter, Nell Irvin. *Exodusters: Black Migration to Kansas After Reconstruction*. New York: W.W. Norton, 1992.

Patton, Pat. Correspondence on Junius Groves, Sr.'s children at Kansas State Agricultural College, June 25, 2012.

Smith, Harlan D. "J.G. Groves," *The American Magazine*, January 1914, 62.

Staab, Rodney. "Junius G. Groves and the African-American Farmers and Potato-Growers of Wyandotte County, Kansas 1830s–1925," *The Consolidated Ethnic History of Wyandotte County*. Kansas City, KS: Kansas Ethnic Council, 2000, 120–48.

St. Louis Republic. "Negro Business Men in Convention," August 17, 1905, 3.

Topeka Plaindealer. "A Potato King," May 4, 1900, 1.

———. "Decline and Fall of Groves' 'Potato Empire' Disclosed as K.P.'s Open Foreclosure Against Estate," February 7, 1930, 1.

———. "Finest Country Home in the West," June 11, 1909, 1.

———. "Potato King's Widow Dies," August 29, 1930, 1.

———. "This Is Negro Enterprise," June 7, 1901, 1.

Truesdale, Jesse. "Crowd Honors 'Potato King' Junius Groves," *The Chieftain,* August 15, 2007.
    www.bonnersprings.com/news/2007/aug/15/crowd_honors_potato/

Untitled, *Historic Times* (Lawrence, Kansas), September 19, 1891, 2.

Washington, Booker T. "Negro Enterprise," *The Outlook,* May 14, 1904, 115–18.

ACKNOWLEDGMENTS

First thanks has to go to my first editor, Nancy Hinkel, who saw the value in Junius G.'s story and his growing of the "humble" potato. For seeing the book through to the finish with so much intelligence and organization, I am so very grateful to my second editor, Julia Maguire. (How many writers are lucky enough to have TWO great editors for their book!)

Thanks is also due to others in editorial—Stephen Brown, Melanie Nolan, and Jennifer Brown; to the designer, Nicole Gastonguay; to the fabulous folks in production; to ace copy editors Artie Bennett and Alison Kolani; to managing editor Dawn Ryan; and to Adrienne Waintraub and Lisa Nadel in school and library marketing. And bushels of thanks to Don Tate!

I am also extremely grateful for tremendous and generous research assists from Tisa M. Anders, independent scholar and founder/CEO, Writing the World, LLC; Susan Boyle, Clerk of the District Court, Kansas City; Nancy W. Burns, Wyandotte County Register of Deeds; Teresa Coble, Kansas State Historical Society; Cliff Hight and Pat Patton, Kansas State University, University Archives; Jennifer Laughlin, Curator, Wyandotte County Museum; Jim Prichard of Louisville, Kentucky, independent researcher; and Angela Doyle Radicia, independent scholar.   —*Tonya Bolden*

In 1884, Junius Groves plopped down a significant sum of money toward the purchase of eighty acres of land east of Edwardsville, Kansas. It was just a down payment, but he and his wife worked the land hard to pay off the difference. The author wrote these scenes so eloquently. And as the illustrator, I was charged with telling the story through pictures—to expand upon the author's text.

I thought the most important thing to communicate was that Junius Groves made good on a promise: he paid what he owed. It's impossible to know exactly what that scene might have looked like 130-something years ago, but my naive style of art—and nonfiction picture books in general—requires some hypotheses. Initially I drew the landowner as a white man.

As I rendered the final illustrations for the book, I wondered about the landowner. What if he was a black man? This scene would have happened two decades after the Civil War, so it was possible. But unlikely. I conferred with the author and found that the landowner was actually a woman named Rosanna Connor. She was Native American, an umbrella term used to reference hundreds of indigenous nations. I was way off!

Surprised at learning this, I decided to do some more research. The land that Junius Groves had purchased was near the Kaw (Kansas) River in Kansas, which was owned by the people of the Kaw Nation at one time. In fact, according to the Kansas Historical Society, the name Topeka, the capital of Kansas, is said to be a Kaw word meaning "a ripe and fertile area" or "a good place to grow potatoes." Double wow!

There weren't any photos of Ms. Connor, and I wanted to avoid any stereotypical representations of her. I asked my friend Cynthia Leitich Smith, who is a member of the Muscogee (Creek) Nation, and I checked with a tribal archivist at the Delaware Tribe of Indians. I also had a conversation with a historian at the Kaw Nation in Kaw City, Oklahoma. Everyone agreed that a Native woman of financial means would have very likely worn a Euro-American style of day dress for business dealings. I had some revising to do.

Since this is the story of Junius Groves, I didn't want to direct the focus of my art away from the subject of this book. But I felt it especially important to make note of the Native American history that pervaded the story of Junius Groves.   —*Don Tate*